D0759858

An Amazing Way to Profit and Prosper Together

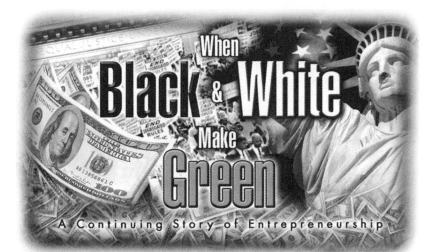

The Next Evolution in
Business & Race

Melvin J. Gravely II, Ph.D.

Edited by Shirley Allen
Illustrations by Gary Dangel
Cover design and inside layout by Ad Graphics, Inc.

Printed in the United States of America.

Gravely, II, Melvin J.,
When Black and White Make Green:
The Next Evolution in Business & Race

ISBN 0-9656194-8-6

Mailing address:
Impact Group Publishers
P.O. Box 621170, Cincinnati, OH 45262-1170

Other Books by
Mel Gravely

The Lost Art of Entrepreneurship
*Rediscovering the Principles That
Will Guarantee Your Success*

Making It Your Business
*The Personal Transition from
Employee to Entrepreneur*

Grandma's Greatest Gifts
Lessons They Shared by Living

ACKNOWLEDGMENTS

To the team of professionals that helped with the research that ultimately became *When Black and White Make Green*. It was truly one of the most rewarding professional experiences of my life. Your level of passion, commitment and your capacity for clear thinking were infectious. Thank you:

- Kevin Armstrong
- Vanessa Freytag
- Arlene Koth
- Rea Waldon

To my wife Chandra. You always know the right words of encouragement.

To my Master Mind group members, Otis Williams and Tammy Wynn. Your critical review always challenges me to think more deeply. Thank you.

To the group of great friends and colleagues who invested many hours reviewing this book and providing valuable input. I am always overwhelmed by your generosity and commitment to me. Thank you all:

Angie Avery, Cliff Bailey, DeAsa Brown, Judy Clark, Tom Cody, Cynthia Cooper, Michael Fisher, Brian Matthews, Sandra Talley, Icy Williams, and Frances Wright.

A special thank you to Arlene Koth. You really do help me hold it all together. Thank you.

TABLE OF CONTENTS

INTRODUCTION

WHAT GOOD
IS THIS BOOK?

This is a different kind of business book. Some reviewers of pre-publication copies have suggested this volume would work best as a traditional, data driven, how-to book. I agree there are some risks to a business book in parable form. However, the book proposes a non-traditional response to an important challenge. I believe that were it delivered in any other way this message would lose its context, its authenticity and its power.

Our mission was to find a new way, a better way, a more significant way to grow sizable minority businesses. Our research team was invited to be bold, innovative and most of all candid about where we are, what we need and what opportunities this mission might present. Many people told us what the solution should be. Everyone had a story and an opinion. At times it was difficult to separate fact from fiction. Our statistical data analysis provided another dimension that added to the texture of our understanding. Most of all our research invited us into a story full of authentic conversations, brutal realities, and new ways of thinking. What we found was that what we have done thus far has created some positive results, but still fails to address the core issues that create the need for special programs. Why are the results not enough? Why does **access** to markets and capital not equal success? Why does race matter? What should we do now? What really is *the next evolution in race and business?*

The concepts from **When Black and White Make Green** are real, based on actual research and ready for your consideration. Most people think that the title refers to the races of black and white. Although that is one application, the broader meaning is that the issues, history and answers are not as clear as *black* and *white*. The title represents the promise that all of our activities, ideas and focus can have the commonality of *green*.

Few topics stir more emotion than issues of race and money and **When Black and White Make Green** is rich with both. It is a quick and entertaining read full of practical ideas that challenge us all to review our programs, our businesses, our processes and, most of all, our thinking. There is a role and a voice for virtually everyone, including corporate leaders, minority business advocates, minority business owners and community leaders. The characters are purely fictional, but do not be surprised to find yourself and others that you know. The aim of this book is to ignite a national conversation about what is next in supplier diversity and economic inclusion.

I invite you to join us in the conversation that starts on the next page.

"We want to make our communities better and more inclusive for all people. But we must be missing something."

1

SOMETHING
HAS TO CHANGE

ax put down his briefcase and sat in the large leather chair in his office at home. He reached for the remote control for the 13-inch TV on a small table against the wall. He turned the channel from ESPN to a local station. The evening news was just starting. "Our breaking story tonight is yet another blow to race relations in The City."

Max turned up the volume. News related to the aftermath of the racial unrest had been the lead story almost every night for the last three months. On one hand, Max was tired of hearing about this stuff, but on the other hand he knew if they stopped the protest, things would probably never change. "The Reverend Alvin Must, spokesman for the Coalition for Racial Justice, has now called for a national boycott of The City. The group is asking that all conventions and events planned for The City move to alternative sites," the newscaster said.

"We are contacting every group that plans to come to The City in the next 18 months. No justice, no money," said the minister as film footage of his image appeared on the screen. "We have heard the promises before but we have seen no results. We have been asked to be patient before, but we have seen no results. The jobless rate, the quality of healthcare, the lack of opportunity for minority businesses all lead to our present state of hopelessness. This boycott is about justice, equality and restoring hope."

The newscaster reappeared, "Although the Coalition for Racial Justice has not made public their specific list of demands, they have made clear their intentions to keep this issue front and center. We will keep you posted. Our next story…"

That's what we need, Max thought. *This is becoming a national story. That's a great image.* Max's office telephone rang. He turned down the volume of the television to answer. "Max Albert," he answered.

"Max this is Don Dressel," the voice on the other end said. "Good evening, Don. How are things?" Max replied.

Don Dressel was the CEO of The City Bank, the largest bank in the region. Max was a bit surprised to hear from Don. He knew him pretty well but he couldn't remember another time he had called him directly.

"Max, I need to talk with you,"

"Sure, what's going on?"

"Have you heard about the national boycott that was just announced?"

"Yes, I just saw it on the evening news."

"Race relations in The City seem to be taking on a life of their own. No matter what we say it doesn't seem to help. In meeting after meeting we've been talking about the racial situation for the last few months. I'm getting frustrated," Don admitted.

"What's frustrating you?"

"A lot of things, but two in particular; first, the knee jerk reactions that I keep seeing coming from people trying to look like they're responding. The reality is that none of what I've seen is ever going to create permanent change."

"Okay," Max remarked to show that he was listening.

"Second is, although I spend most of my time these days talking about these issues, I really don't understand them. I appreciate that people are angry, frustrated and even hurting but I really don't know what is at the root of it all."

"Hmm."

"I've been meeting with a small group of CEOs in The City about the state of race relations. What we quickly realized was that our views about race are pretty much the same." Don admitted.

"What view is that, Don?"

"Max, we wonder what more they want? We think we've already done so much."

Max was silent.

Don continued, "We've developed work and supplier diversity programs. We've all given to minority causes like the Urban League and the NAACP. Look at the budgets of those groups. Calculate how much of it comes from major corporations. We've championed efforts to make sure minorities have an opportunity to participate on the building of the new convention center, the new ballpark, the new library and the new history museum."

"Yeah, you're right" Max added reluctantly.

"Max, you know that the various non-profit boards have never been more diverse. We've all worked to diversify our boards of directors with both women and minorities. The City now has multiple minority chambers of commerce and a minority business incubator. All of them funded and often times staffed by our major corporations."

"Despite everything you said we are still not making very much progress."

"See, I think we've made significant progress in many areas," Don replied.

Max was not sure what progress Don was talking about, but progress had been limited and extremely slow to come.

I could challenge him on things like minorities on his board of directors or in senior levels of his company or how much business they do with minority suppliers, Max thought. So much of his conversation was accurate that Max thought it was best to let him keep venting.

"How much is enough?" Don continued. "When does it stop being all our fault? Minorities have access. They have assistance programs. What else can we do? People say they want more opportunity, but so many times we struggle to find minority businesses that are ready."

"I agree with a lot of what you're saying. The system is broken and, despite what you think are your best efforts, minorities still aren't happy. I'm frustrated too. I'm not sure what the remedies are but I'm sure that something is going to have to change," Max replied.

"I agree. We want to help. We want to make our communities better and more inclusive for all people. But we must be missing something. What we need most is a better view and a clearer vision of how we can improve things. Our small group of CEOs is particularly interested in the state of minority business in The City. We want to understand it better and determine how we can really start making a difference that people realize and value. I know it's short notice, but can you meet with us in the morning to provide your insight on how we might go about doing that?"

Max paused for a moment to collect his thoughts. He was flattered to be called by Don but was a bit skeptical of the real intention.

"I'm not sure what type of insight you think I might be able to provide," Max replied.

"We're not sure either. But Max, we do know that we have a problem. We know we can't help with a solution if we don't even know what the problem is. I'm sure you're getting pulled in all kinds of directions on this issue. Just give me one meeting and see how it goes," Don said.

It was as close to pleading as Max had ever heard from a corporate executive.

"OK," Max conceded.

"Great. We've been meeting at 7:30 a.m. at The City Club downtown," Don explained.

"That sounds fine. I'll see you then," Max concluded.

The two men hung up.

"Man, this has really gotten bad," Max said aloud. "These boycotters may have struck a nerve. The challenge will be turning all of this attention into results."

CHAPTER
2

THIS IS BIGGER THAN "A LITTLE UNREST"

It was early. Max was already on his way downtown. People always complained about the commute times around The City. But the early morning was different. Max enjoyed the early morning and the 30 minute drive downtown. He looked at the landscape of his adopted hometown and realized that he still loved living here. He had been in The City for 15 years, and he still loved the quality of life, the people and the opportunities. The City had been good for him and his family. It bothered him that race relations had become the center of what The City was known for.

His cellular telephone rang. "Max Albert," he answered after pushing the button on the center of his steering wheel.

"Hey, Max, this is Miguel," the voice said.

"Hey Miguel. What's going on?" Max replied.

"Max, I just wanted to touch base with you to make sure you got the paperwork I sent you about the new lake front development."

"Yeah, I got it. Thanks for keeping me informed. It looks like a great project for The City," Max said.

"It's a great project but I'm not sure it'll work in this town."

"What do you mean *this town*?" Max questioned.

"I'm just getting tired, Max," Miguel said. "I've been an attorney in this city for 18 years. I grew up here. The people know me. I went to the *right* schools. I serve on the *right* boards. I give to the *right* causes and I still feel like I'll never really break through. Like I'll never really be included. I have to admit that I'm getting pretty frustrated and even angry."

Max and Miguel were good friends. Miguel was one of the first people Max met when he came to town. Miguel was responsible for helping Max get connected in town. He was a good guy, a levelheaded thinker and a respected attorney. He was one of the most involved community volunteers Max had ever met.

"What's really going on, Miguel?"

"I'm not sure" Miguel replied. "These folks just don't get it. They think this racial unrest is about a few uneducated brothas throwing stuff on the square. They just don't get it. This is much bigger than that. Man, the best and brightest people of color are just as frustrated."

Max just listened.

"I sit in meetings with people now and you can just tell. Folks are tired of working and waiting and not making any progress. Having a seat on a board of directors without any real voice is getting old. What's the use if you can't make a difference? It's just getting old, man."

"Man, you *are* frustrated," Max replied. "What brought this on?"

"I'm not sure. There's no doubt that the racial unrest brought it all up. The City's response to the situation didn't help. But Max, what bothers me most is their lack of acknowledgement that *race does matter*. I went to the *right* law school, worked in the *right* law firms, volunteer twice as much as my peers and I'm good at what I do. I've paid my dues and I've heard the promises but my question is *where's the file?* If I'm such a val-ued community resource, with all of the right connections, where is the file? Why are my peers that went to The City University School of Law, with less experience and less com-munity involvement, farther ahead than I am?"

Max wasn't sure what *the file* meant but Miguel was on a roll and the details didn't seem important to the point he was making. The point was he thought he should be far-ther along. The point was that despite his high level of involvement, he still didn't feel included. He was frustrated to a point of anger.

"Maybe it's just the working too hard for too long and get-ting too little. I don't know, but I'm telling you, I've never seen it this way. Did you hear about the meeting yesterday morning?" Miguel asked.

"Yes, I was invited but I got back to town too late," Max replied. "How did it go?"

"Man, it was the most moving meeting I've ever attended. Forty of the who's who of the minority business leaders of The City were there. I have to get out of here for a meeting so I don't have time to go into detail but in essence they agreed to push for and see change soon or 'secede from the Union.'"

Max chuckled. "What do you mean secede from the Union?"

"I mean secede. These folks are committed to improving the plight of minorities in this city or resigning from all boards and even moving their businesses. They have agreed to disconnect with The City."

"Are you serious?" Max questioned.

"Very serious. Something has to change, Max," Miguel replied.

"Do you think that will help?" asked Max.

"I don't know but I think people are so fed up that they feel they have no other choice. We've been playing this game long enough. We've heard the promises and seen them broken. We've served on the committees and seen them do nothing new. We're not sure we're even making progress but if we are we have to *accelerate the pace*."

"Man…," Max said not knowing what else to say.

"Hey, we can talk about this more later. I have to get going," Miguel said.

"OK, I'll talk to you later," Max replied.

Max pushed the red end key on his steering wheel. He was in a daze. Miguel was a good guy and typically one of his most conservative friends. If he was this upset, what were others thinking?

Max exited the highway, turned right and pulled into The City Club parking lot.

"Good morning, Mr. Albert" the valet said.

"Good morning, Danny. Has Don Dressel arrived yet?" Max asked.

"Yes. He and his party got here about three minutes ago."

Max looked at his watch. He was about five minutes early. *Perfect* he thought. He really did hate to be late. He reached into his back seat to remove his suit jacket from the hanger and put it on. Danny handed him his briefcase and his claim ticket and Max walked into the club.

"We have all spent what we think is a lot of money in supplier diversity and minority purchasing and it's obviously not been enough."

CHAPTER
3

WHAT CAN WE DO?

"Max, how are you?" Don asked as he and three other men rose from a large round table.

Max smiled, "Good morning gentlemen," he said comfortably.

He knew every one of them. This was the elite of the business executives of The City. All of them were CEOs of Fortune 500 companies — Don Dressel from the Bank, John Stevens of Venture Steel, Bob Grum of The City Power and Gas, and Rob Mindel of VanHunt Financial.

The men all sat down. The waiter poured Max a cup of coffee and silently placed a creamer next to him.

John Stevens spoke first. "Max, we appreciate your coming this morning. We need you."

"That's always good to hear," Max joked, looking up from his cup of coffee.

The men smiled. John continued, "We want to make things better in this community. We want to do what we can to improve race relations and more importantly we want to help The City be known as a place that provides real opportunity for *everyone*."

Max nodded. He had no idea where this was all going.

"There are a lot of other initiatives going on in response to the riots of a few months ago. Our companies are involved and will continue to be," John said, taking a sip from his coffee.

Rob Mindel cleared his throat and spoke, "We think that one of our biggest opportunities to create real and systemic change is through the development of a more vibrant minority entrepreneurial environment."

"We think we're already making progress but it doesn't appear we're making it fast enough or in ways that are visible. We need your help to figure out how to *accelerate the pace* of progress," Don Dressel added. "We need you to help us figure out a plan of action that will work."

"Well, that's straight to the point," Max said.

"Well, we've been talking about this for some time now. More businesses mean more jobs, more jobs mean better neighborhoods, improved schools, and most of all an increased level of hope," Don said.

"Why entrepreneurship? Why not job creation or board representation or any of the many other approaches you could support?" Max asked.

"We are involved in many of those things but there are good reasons why we think improvements in minority entrepreneurship could make the ultimate difference. First, entrepreneurship is the only initiative that has the potential to affect all of the other things you just mentioned. From politics to job creation to healthcare, building minority wealth through entrepreneurship can positively impact them all."

Don paused to look at his peers around the table for their agreement. He continued.

"Second, minority entrepreneurship can increase the economic pie for the entire community. The more successful businesses we have, irrespective of their race, the better it is for all of us. You know me — I'm always looking for more good bank customers. Third, entrepreneurship is the bedrock of our country. Improvements here don't feed people; they teach them to fish. Long-term, that may be the only approach that will last. The fourth reason we believe we should focus on minority entrepreneurship is the fact that we're uniquely positioned to really make an impact on this area. Collectively...," he said leaning back and spreading his arms "we're a pretty large customer base," Don concluded.

Max nodded. "I understand what you want to accomplish but I'm still unclear what you want from me," Max said.

"We're not sure either," Bob Grum replied. "We want you to decide what you need to do and then do it."

"Why me? There are people in The City that have spent their lives working in the area of minority business development. Wouldn't they be better candidates?" Max said.

"Maybe they would but we doubt it," Steve replied. "We think we would get the same old type of approach we have today."

"This has to be different from anything we have seen before. We want something that is not a give-away, something that is market driven and leads to economic development in the form of jobs, taxes and home ownership. We have all spent what we think is a lot of money in supplier diversity and minority purchasing and it's obviously not been enough. We don't want to keep spending and spending and hear that things have not really changed," Rob Mindel added.

"We know you, Max. What you come up with will have credibility with our peers and with those in the minority community. You've moved through the system before. You have lived the life. You know what it takes," Don added.

"We'll make sure you have the resources you need. Don't worry about that," Rob Mindel said. "What do you say?"

"Let me consider what we've talked about. I like the idea and I agree that minority entrepreneurship has a chance to really create change. I want to talk to a few of my advisors. I'll get back to you in the next few days."

Max took one last sip from his coffee cup and moved his chair back to leave. Everyone rose from the table. The men all exchanged handshakes and walked down the hall to the elevator together chatting about the topics of the day.

Max's mind wandered. He thought it was interesting that in one morning he heard two different conversations, from two different points of view but both wanted the same things...*to accelerate the pace.* The City Club elevator reached the first floor, the men exited and walked their separate ways.

"But you can never forget about the historical baggage that issues of race carry."

CHAPTER
4

DO YOU CARE
THAT MUCH?

Max pulled his car into The Country Club parking lot. He was excited because he had not seen his most valued advisor for months. There had not been the need to get together since Max had sold his valve manufacturing business. Hugh had been a constant and stable fixture in Max's life for more than 10 years. His advice was typically challenging but always valuable.

Max was dressed casually. He could see Hugh already seated at a table in the casual dining room.

Hugh rose slowly to shake Max's hand, "Good day, young man," Hugh said.

"Hugh, thanks for agreeing to meet with me."

"No problem, Max. I miss our talks and the excitement of being with you as you ran your business. That kind of stuff keeps me young."

Max could never tell how old Hugh really was. He looked to be close to 100 years old but his wisdom even surpassed those years. It was amazing that Hugh never seemed to age.

"This one is nothing like running my business, Hugh. Did you get the gist of what they want me to do?"

"Yes, Max, I think I get it."

"Well, should I?" Max asked.

"Should you what?"

"Should I try to help figure out how to develop a more vibrant minority entrepreneurial environment?"

"Oh, I don't know. Should you?"

"Come on, Hugh. Help me out here."

"Max, I'm not here to answer your questions for you. You know that. But I will ask you one."

"Go ahead."

"Do you care?"

"Yes, I care. I love The City and I believe in minority entrepreneurship and I think we have to get some things done that will really impact the style and level of economic inclusion of minorities."

"Now that was an answer. Do you mean it?" Hugh pressed.

"Of course I do," Max answered. "But I really don't know what to tell them. If I were honest, my personal success was a complex mix of situations over time that I'm not sure I could even make sense of."

"Max, your own personal experience is only one dimension of why they have asked you for help. It's a rare person that maintains credibility and respect across a wide spectrum of the population. They did not ask you because of what you already know. They asked you because they know you will communicate with all sides and deliver an authentic answer."

Hugh was right. Max had worked hard to maintain his relationships with people in the entire community.

"The only question, Max, is do you want to do it bad enough to deal with the stuff you'll have to deal with?"

"What stuff? They were very clear that they would provide the resources I need."

"Maybe they will. But that is not what I'm talking about. Max, this is not just another community project like children reading by age six or making The City a national technology hub or trying to increase tourism. There is never an uproar about those types of issues. But people have strong feelings about race. Everyone has an opinion and most people think they're experts. There will be those who think the whole idea is yet another give-away program for people who have not made good decisions in their lives. Others will see it as reverse discrimination. You've heard it. 'Why should we just help minority businesses grow? I could use the help too.'"

Max just listened.

"What you have described to me could be something different and maybe even the right next thing to do as it relates to minority business development. But you can never forget about the historical baggage that issues of race carry. This will take a lot of heavy lifting. Do you care THAT much?"

"I don't know, Hugh. I just know this one feels special. The CEOs in that room seemed to be committed. The interaction felt real."

"That's great for now. But what happens when your solutions don't match with their plans or when what you find requires them and their organizations to change the way they do business? Your interactions are all good now but by the very nature of what you have to do you will be in a position of asking fixed objects to move and change. Do you care THAT much?"

Max sat silently pondering Hugh's words. He was right. If they want something different from what we already have, it will mean that things will have to change. Max knew people did not like change, and especially changes in deeply rooted beliefs. Race really is one of those super charged issues and this was about race *and* money. Man, it just doesn't get much more charged than that. *But if not me, who?* he thought.

"Hugh, this is one of those rare opportunities that you feel like your entire life has made you ready for. This one is too important not to do. I have to take it on."

"Max, I figured you would," Hugh said as he reached into the inside pocket of his jacket that was hanging on the back of his chair. "Here, these folks might be able to help."

He handed Max a sheet of paper that was folded lengthwise. "Go ahead, open it," Hugh said.

There were three names on the paper with the contact information for each.

"These are the smartest thinkers I know. Dionne has her finger on the most current data. Megan really understands programs and program development. Will is young but he really brings a balanced understanding of minority issues. They know how to work well on teams and how to get things done. I have already told them that you may be calling."

Hugh stood up from the table to leave.

"It's OK if you don't use them. This is your baby. I know you have what it takes to give The City the type of outcome that will really matter. Call me if you need me."

Max sat at the table alone for a moment. He reached for his cellular phone and called Don Dressel, the bank CEO. "Don, this is Max Albert...."

"There are already too many programs out there with the same mission. Why do people think we need another one?"

CHAPTER

5

MEETING THE TEAM

H ugh *really has some serious relationships with people,* Max thought. Every one of the people he recommended for the team said "yes" without hesitation when Max called. He didn't even have to explain much about the work that was to be done. When they heard the name Hugh, they were ready to sign up.

Max was excited as he approached one of his office buildings.

"Good morning, Mr. Albert," the receptionist said as Max walked into the lobby. "Your meeting is in the Mount Union conference room. Ms. Kalm and your guests are waiting."

"Thanks, Phyllis," Max responded. Max smiled. He sort of missed being in this environment everyday. Although he still owned the building and had a small office here, he was no longer in the mix of the day-to-day work of the company. Ms. Kalm had worked with Max since the beginning. They were now more like partners and she was a master at organizing people.

"Well, good morning." Max said as he entered the Mount Union conference room.

"Good morning," the people in the room said in unison. They stood to greet him. A petite Black woman was first, "Hello, Max, I'm Dionne. My friends call me Data."

"Hi, I'm Megan. I don't have a nickname," the next lady said smiling. She was a casually dressed White woman with a firm handshake and a confident manner.

A trim, average height man was last. Max could not help but notice how young he looked. "Hello, I'm William. Call me Will." The two men shook hands.

"You have already met Ms. Kalm and I'm Max Albert. Thank you all for coming. You come highly recommended and I'm excited you have agreed to help us."

"Don't believe a word Hugh says," Dionne responded.

They all laughed.

"Dionne, Hugh rarely gets it wrong."

Megan spoke next, "Max, Hugh didn't tell us much. What are we helping with?"

"Our mission is to develop a plan to *accelerate the pace* of progress of minority business development in The City," Max responded.

"There are already too many programs out there with the same mission. Why do people think we need another one?" Dionne asked.

"Dionne, I mean Data," he said smiling, "that's a great question. Finding the answer to that question is a part of our first step. We have been commissioned and financed by the top CEOs in The City. I know them and I'm sure they already have an idea of what they want. We cannot let what they want stop us from finding good solutions. We're working for our entire community."

The group just listened.

"How much time do we have?" Kalm asked.

"Based on how things are going, we don't have much. I've heard that a group of the most influential minority business leaders are planning to resign from every board in The City if they don't see significant signs of progress in the next six months. The implications for our national image could take years to repair but they are just fed up with waiting," Will reported.

"That's OK, I don't think that the CEOs are any less frustrated. They're getting sick of being blamed for all the problems, especially since they think they've already done so much. Nothing seems to be enough. They are close to giving up too," Megan added.

"The state of race relations in The City is bad and getting worse. Everyone wants to see progress and they want to see it now. We only have six months before the minority business leaders fulfill their promise to quit their involvement in The City and maybe even less before the CEOs give up trying. We need to do our work in 90 days," Max said.

"Ninety days to do, at the very least, nine months of work? That just makes it more fun," Dionne said.

The others nodded and moved closer to the conference room table. "We better get started," Megan suggested.

"Sounds like we're ready," Max said as he stood to move to the flip chart stand in the corner of the conference room. He flipped the sheet of paper over and began to draw a diagram.

"We have a lot of data to gather. Dionne, will you put together our statistical review? Find out where we are right now. How well are we doing? How are other communities doing and who is doing the best?" Max requested.

"Sure. They don't call me Data for nothing."

"Megan, will you examine other programs around The City and around the country. Let's find out what's working, what isn't and why."

"No problem."

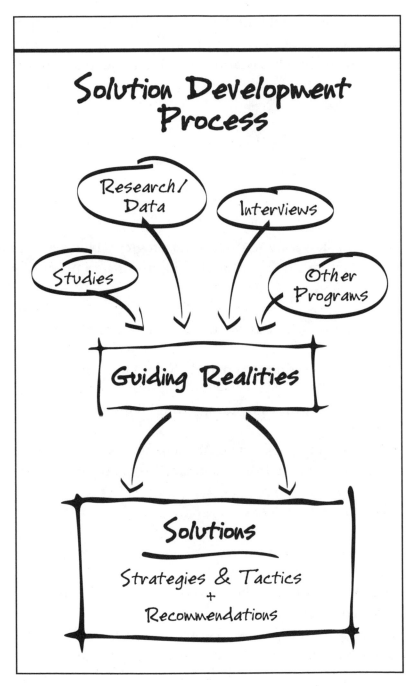

WhenBlack and White MakeGreen

"Will, you and I will lead the effort to interview key people. Ladies, we will need your help with particular interviews where you might have relationships. How does that sound?"

"That's good."

"Kalm, can you arrange the logistics for the interviews and data collection?"

"Got it."

"We will talk weekly to discuss our progress. The goal is to be prepared to present your findings to this group during our next meeting."

Everyone had their head down busily taking a few final notes.

"Hey, this project needs a name," Kalm said.

"I was thinking the same thing," said Dionne.

"I was thinking about 'The Accelerator,'" Kalm explained moving her hands in front of her face. "What do you think?"

"I love that," Megan said.

"That's catchy," Will added.

"'The Accelerator' it is then," Max proclaimed. "Ladies and gentleman, we have a chance to do something special here. We all have some base of knowledge on this topic. Our knowledge can help us but it can also get in our way. We must find a way not to let what we already know and believe impede us from finding breakthrough solutions. No answer is wrong if it furthers our cause. We don't have time to ponder the politics of being polite. Everyone out there will have opinions and suggestions to consider. Many of them will be promising but outside the scope of what we are charged to do. Stay focused. We only have 90 days. Any questions?" Max concluded.

No one had any.

"Great! We will get together again as a group in about a month. That should give us enough time to perform the interviews, review other programs and collect the needed data. Kalm will send out minutes from this meeting and a reminder for the next."

Everyone grabbed their things and began to move toward the door. Max collected his things slowly as he smiled. *This really is a very good team*, he thought. *It's time to find some real solutions.*

"...we have failed to make any significant impact in this area. Whatever we do just doesn't seem to be enough."

CHAPTER

6

PLEASE, NOT
ANOTHER PROGRAM

Max was on his way to interview Bob Smitherman. Bob was known for being one of the most *conservative* of the local CEOs. Most people would put Bob in the category of executives who *don't get it*. Don Dressel and the other CEOs felt it was important not only to get Bob's input, but to get his support for whatever this whole thing was going to become. Max took this interview himself because he knew Bob. They had served on the United Way Board together. Max also knew this could end up being a very difficult conversation.

Max was almost downtown when his cell phone rang.

"Max Albert," he answered.

"Max, this is Miguel. I only have one question. Is it true?"

"Is what true?" Max asked.

"Is it true you're going to let them use you?"

"What are you talking about, Miguel? Use me to do what?"

"They are going to use you and all you have done to make it look like they care. You're going to help them create more promises and show no results." Miguel said. "Max, we have seen enough programs. We don't need another one."

"Miguel, aren't you the one that told me you wanted to see things change? You even warned me that if things don't change folks were going to secede from their participation in The City. How can things change if things don't change?"

Miguel was quiet.

"How can we know what will really make things better without taking an honest look? It's going to take more than getting pissed off to make something happen."

"Max, you're working for them."

"Miguel, if you really believe that, I'll never convince you otherwise. I guess we'll just have to see."

"Don't sell us out, Max."

"Miguel, I've got to tell you that I'm offended by your comments. I'm really trying to listen to what you're telling me but it's difficult. Listen, man, I have to get to a meeting and I'm headed into a parking deck. I'll talk to you later."

"What was that about?" Max said aloud shaking his head. "How do we make progress without doing something?"

Max parked his car, grabbed his jacket and headed to Bob's office.

"Good morning, I'm Max Albert. I'm here to see Bob Smitherman."

"Yes, Mr. Albert. Bob is expecting you. Go right in."

Max entered the sizable office. It was large but much less impressive than Max expected. It was furnished with dated furniture and pictures and awards lined the blandly colored walls.

Bob came from behind his desk, "Good morning, Max," he said reaching out his hand.

"Good morning, Bob. Thanks for meeting with me."

"No problem, Max. The other CEOs are talking about the work you and your team are doing. I'm very interested in hearing more about it."

Bob pointed to a seat at the small conference table inviting Max to sit.

"Bob, our mission is to develop an approach to accelerate the pace of development of minority businesses in The City. We're talking to various segments of our community to seek a thorough understanding of the dynamics that contribute to our current state."

"Max, we have no fewer than ten programs designed to develop minority businesses. My corporation and many others in The City give thousands of dollars to this cause every year. Most of the programs seem to be doing very little, but we have to keep supporting them to protect our companies from becoming front-page news. No corporation wants to be caught not supporting minority issues these days. So the obvious question is, why do we need another program?"

"Bob, I think you're making the point for the purpose of our work. Why is what we're currently doing not getting us the results we expect?"

"The question is bigger than that. I wonder should we still be doing so much for a particular group based on race. What about the thousands of other business owners that no one is doing anything for? Should we have special programs for them too?"

"I think there are many people who share your question. I must admit that I don't know all of the answers. But our focus is on the benefits of accelerating our progress. We believe that accelerating the growth of minority businesses is a community-wide economic development opportunity."

Bob smiled. "Economic development opportunity? Is that the pitch now?"

Max smiled too. "I am not sure I'd call it a *pitch*. It really does follow from a strong foundation of facts."

Bob laughed.

Max laughed too. "Really, Bob. Think about it. The minority population is growing faster than that of whites. The census data is clear. People over the age of 70 have a 20% chance of being a person of color. Children under the age of 10 have a 75% chance. That's quite a shift."

"OK, that's true."

"We also know that minority unemployment is significantly higher than the average."

"Yes, but there are so many different reasons for that unemployment figure."

"Sure there are, but the fact still remains that these people are on the fringe of the economic system. Many are not substantial contributors. And despite all the reasons for unemployment, minority businesses hire more minorities than other companies. Following through on that logic, the more sizable minority businesses, the more employed minorities. The net effect is more people contributing to the economy."

"That sounds good in theory, Max, but we have heard these propositions before."

"I agree, Bob, and that's our challenge. How do we make this promise real?"

Bob nodded.

"You know this issue also affects your company directly. If The City is not seen as inclusive and accepting of diversity, we struggle to bring top talent here."

"Now *that* I agree with. We are developing an image problem that is affecting our recruiting efforts, especially among minorities," Bob conceded.

"The Convention and Visitors' Bureau suggests that this image problem spills over into tourism and convention business too," Max added. "Not only do minority groups not want to come to The City, but other groups don't want to come here either. This is certainly an economic development issue."

"I understand the theory, Max, but I hope you agree that we have failed to make any significant impact in this area. Whatever we do just doesn't seem to be enough," Bob said.

"The potential benefits are worth the effort. Employing more of the most systemically unemployed means better schools, better neighborhoods, more homeowners and more consumers. It also means an environment of inclusion that will help our politics, philanthropy and our community image," Max presented.

"The issue is that you're asking for an investment now. The benefits are future based and we have no experiences to rely on to *believe* the benefits have a chance of happening," Bob said.

"What's so unusual about that?" Max asked raising his voice slightly. "Most of the investments corporations make are based on the expectation of benefits in the future."

"This one is different because you're asking me to invest in a group I have very little influence over. That alone makes the investment different from typical corporate investments."

Max just nodded.

"So what questions do you have for me?" Bob asked seeming tired of the theoretical banter.

"The big question is, what do you think stands in the way of our community having more successful minority businesses?"

"Max, business is business. Our corporation and most of our peer organizations have a focus on developing a diverse supplier base. The big issue is that we can't find the type of firms that can compete for our business. The minority firms are too often too small and in businesses that are ancillary to our core business."

Max took notes on his pad.

"I think we have enough access for these businesses. I think we may have hurt them by lowering our expectations for what we need from them. Now when I think strategic supplier, I don't think minority because my perception is they're not ready. The groups in the business of developing minority businesses often push the same notion," Bob said.

"What do you mean?" Max asked.

"When a group tells you that a minority business needs a lower interest rate on a loan, or access to free consulting, or they push for legislation that mandates a particular percent of the business go to a minority, all of this leads to the conclusion that these businesses can not compete."

Max did not like what Bob was saying. It felt like he was attacking current programs and Max had grown his business in this very environment. In some ways Bob was talking about him. The two men talked for a few more minutes before Max left.

CHAPTER
7

REALITY –
IT IS WHAT IT IS

Max had just completed his last interview. He was driving back home thinking about what he had heard and anticipating the information he would get from the others the next day. A month had passed and the time had gone quickly. Max was beginning to feel the burden of putting everything together. He looked at his watch. *This is Hugh's time at the park,* he thought. Max took a quick right hand turn and parked his car on the street.

He grabbed his jacket and walked toward the park bench that Hugh occupied every Thursday at this time. He and Hugh had spent days and days in this park talking about how business really worked and the personal principles of entrepreneurial success. Max used to think the park was a strange place to meet. Now he thought it was the perfect environment to really relax and think clearly and deeply.

He could see Hugh seated on the bench. Birds were all around him.

"Well, Max, this is a surprise," Hugh said without looking up.

Hugh's greeting startled Max a little. "I just thought I would drop in and give you an update on the progress of The Accelerator project."

"The Accelerator. Hmm, nice name. Sit down. I'm all ears," Hugh said patting the seat next to him and handing Max a small bag of birdseed.

"I just finished the last interview," Max said

"And?" Hugh inquired.

"Hugh it's been 40 years since the Civil Rights movement and I'm not sure how far we've come. How did things get this way?"

"Max, I think you need a little history refresher. The Civil Rights movement has become just a title for a time gone by. People seem to have forgotten that the Civil Rights movement was a politically driven social solution. The outcomes were laws, and guidelines and goals. What is most important to remember is that the focus was on access. Access to schools, corporate jobs, and yes, access for minority businesses. It was all about access."

Max just listened.

"What you're seeing right now is the outcome of the fact that most of our approaches in minority business development are still about access."

"Do the access programs still have a role?" Max asked.

"Access programs have an important role. Access is important; even fundamental. A better question might be, is it time to go a step higher in the hierarchy of solutions? Maybe it is time to consider the more complex issues too."

"Complexity. That's it. That's what I'm feeling, Hugh. The rest of the team will deliver their results tomorrow and from what they tell me they have massive amounts of data. There are so many issues to discuss. So many factors that contribute to our current state. So many points of view, agendas and bias. It's just a lot."

"I bet," Hugh said. "But what you've collected is not what's actually going on. It's the outcomes and impressions of what's going on. Those are the programs that got us to this place, the attitudes that surround the issues of the day, the frustrations of years of trying and a perception that nothing is really changing. All of this input seems to tell you so much, but in a vacuum, means very little."

"What do you mean it means little? We conducted over 40 interviews, evaluated 30 different programs, and reviewed over 22 related studies and data sources," Max said.

"Most of the data you gathered will suggest that our current approach is not working. I hate to tell you this, Max, but most people already agree it's not working, especially the people you'll be talking with. We just differ on the reasons why and what should be done to make things work better."

Hugh leaned forward on the bench seat.

"Max, most people want a just and fair world and those few that don't, don't really matter. Whatever you do, don't act on the perceptions. Don't *react* to what is going on now. Figure out how it should work, consider why it isn't working that way and generate your plan from there. Somewhere in the interaction of all that your team has discovered is a small set of three or four realities. Look for the realities."

"The realities," Max said quietly. The two men just sat quietly on the bench. Hugh continued to feed the birds. Max just sat.

Hugh cleared his throat and spoke, "Max, I want you to be careful with your next steps. There will be many competing interests, many opportunities, and even more distractions. Your challenge will be to pull together the best solution to address the realities."

Max just looked at Hugh, trying to take in what he was saying.

"Remember these five things as you go forward. 1. Focus. Figure out what piece of the puzzle you are going to address and address it. You're going to have to find a way to be OK not trying to fix it all. 2. Make it doable. A plan is great but it's just a plan until you act. Make the plan realistic and actionable so that people will have the expectation that something is going to happen. 3. Make it new – Avoid the issues that have plagued other attempts to improve minority entrepreneurship. Steer away from solutions that place the blame and the responsibility for fixing it on one side or the other. No one group made this reality happen. There must be a significant commitment from all sides. 4. Make it sustainable – The closer your plan is to the natural laws of business, the easier it will be to sustain. 5. Don't crush history. Honor the programs and approaches of the past. They were and maybe are the way things are done. You don't need to tear anything else down to make your approach look good."

Max repeated the five things to himself. *Focus. Make it doable. Make it new. Make it sustainable. Don't crush history.*

Hugh began to gather his things and make his way to his feet. "I have to go, young man, and you have a lot of work to do. Call me if you need me or just come by here on Thursday afternoon. I'll be here."

"Thanks, Hugh, I'm going to sit here for a while. I'll talk with you later."

Hugh walked away slowly. Max leaned back on the bench and lifted his arms behind his head. *Man, do we have a lot of work to do*, he said to himself.

He pulled out his cellular phone and dialed, "Kalm, this is Max. I need a few things for tomorrow's meeting...."

"I think all of these programs and the promotion of the programs have changed the natural dynamics of business."

CHAPTER
8

WHERE ARE WE NOW AND HOW DID WE GET HERE?

Max turned the corner and entered the Mount Union Conference room. No one was there yet, but the room was set up just as he had requested. There were three posters hanging on the walls. One said "Mission: To *accelerate* the progress of minority business development." Another said "The Plan Must... be focused, be doable, be new, be sustainable and not crush history." The third poster said "Key Questions: Where are we now? What are others doing? What do our findings mean? What should we do?"

Max put his things down on the conference table.

Kalm walked in next. "Max, how do they look?" she asked.

"They look great. Thanks. I think we're ready," Max replied.

One by one the other team members entered the room. At nine o'clock sharp Max called the meeting to order.

The Plan Must...

...be focused

...be doable

...be new

...be sustainable

...not crush history

"Thank you all for coming back," Max said smiling. "As you have noticed, Kalm has had a few posters made to help keep us on track. I talked to each of you about these ideas yesterday. I hope you had at least a little time to give them some thought. Are there any questions or comments before we start going through the findings of the various research we all did?"

"No questions, but I do want to thank you for the coffee. Me and mornings just can't get along and the coffee definitely helps," Dionne said stifling a yawn.

The group chuckled.

"We're glad to have you with us, Data," Max said with a wide grin. "Our rough agenda for today," Max said, standing to write on the flip chart, "is to review the findings of Dionne's data research, then talk about what Megan found in her review of other programs, then we can all contribute to what we got from the many interviews and we will conclude this meeting discussing what all of this means. How does that sound?"

Max paused to look around the table for everyone's agreement. "Well, Dionne, since you're awake now, will you talk about the data you found about where we are right now."

Dionne spent the next hour presenting her findings. She talked about the number of minority businesses, their percent contribution to total sales, and average number of employees. She presented local and national numbers. She also compared The City to cities that had similar demographics, cities that were close in proximity and cities that were seen as being the best for minority businesses.

"Man, the numbers don't look good," observed Will

"No, they don't look good. The numbers for even the best cities aren't good. That's a lot of data, but what does it mean?" Max asked.

"There are at least three clear conclusions: 1. There are too few sizable minority businesses to provide any significant capacity or ability to be a significant supplier. This makes capacity a major issue. I believe our focus should be on accelerating the growth in the number of sizable minority-owned businesses. 2. Minority-owned businesses have limited inclusion in the local economy of The City. For example, their percent of total sales is so low it barely registers. 3. Minorities are less likely to own asset-based businesses. Minority businesses driven by tangible assets like equipment, machinery and commercial property are rare. I really believe this makes them less scalable and less attractive to capital sources."

"Good work, Data, and a good summary," Max said.

"I agree. That's really good work and it's also very interesting," Megan commented, clearly thinking. "Especially based on the amount of effort, the dollars being spent and the number of programs we found whose mission it is to develop minority businesses."

"Megan, go ahead and bring us up to speed on what you found out about other programs around the country," Max said.

"This whole thing was quite eye opening. I looked at programs from government and quasi government organizations,

Conclusion of Data Review

1. There are too few sizable minority businesses.

2. Minority-owned businesses have limited inclusion in the local economy.

3. Minorities are less likely to own asset-based businesses.

foundations and non-profits and major corporations. I reviewed programs for technical assistance, supplier diversity and access to capital." Megan paused for a moment to organize her thoughts. "The programs focused on what I call *the sacred trilogy of minority business development*; access to markets, access to capital and access to managerial and technical assistance."

"The sacred trilogy of minority business development?" Will asked.

"Yes, *the sacred trilogy* is the accepted givens in the world of minority business development. The common thought is that every problem can be solved by providing more access," Dionne added.

"That seems pretty simplistic," Will said.

Dionne just shrugged her shoulders.

"We learned four things from the programs that seemed to be getting the best results: 1. Successful programs incorporate several methodologies. They don't just rely on effecting one of the sacred trilogies with one approach. 2. Successful programs need an environment that supports the inclusion of minorities. It was clear that the best results were found in environments that talked about, committed resources to and generally made this topic important. 3. Top-level support and leadership are critical. From the mayor, to the top CEOs, to community leaders, all must demonstrate their support. 4. Competitive advantage is the best motivation to create these programs," Megan continued.

Conclusion of Program Review

Successful programs...

...incorporate several methodologies

...need an environment that supports inclusion

...need top-level support and leadership

...are motivated by a desire for competitive advantage

"Whose competitive advantage?" Dionne asked.

"Organizations and communities that did the best job accelerating minority business believed they would be better because of it. The best programs were started to make the corporations or the communities more competitive. For example, communities pursued minority business development because they believed they would be more attractive communities in which to live and work. They thought they would improve their tax base, their home ownership rates, their public school systems and the general quality of life. The best corporate programs are run by corporations who believe that developing minority businesses would be able to do things like develop more loyal customers, be able to lower their cost, and attract a more talented workforce. The motivation in these cases was not a social one but one of competing in the market," explained Megan.

"So you think the motivation for the programs matters in the effectiveness of the program?" Max asked.

"Yes, I do. If the motivation is driven by market competitiveness, the programs get the commitment and resources that they need," Megan answered.

"That really is no different than any other investment," Max concluded.

"You know, the motivation of competitive advantage came through in the interviews too," Will added.

"I heard it too. It came up again and again," said Dionne.

The others all nodded in agreement.

Megan continued. "There was one more consistent but surprising theme of the many programs we reviewed. With the exception of programs that helped with getting contracts and supplier diversity, the programs to assist minority businesses were greatly underutilized."

"Underutilized?" asked Will.

"Yes, they were wanting for participants," Megan said, leaning up to make her point. "For example, everyone talks about a need for capital but many of the capital funds focused on minorities reported having trouble finding minority deals to fund. The technical assistance programs were just as poorly utilized, if not worse."

Max leaned back in his chair and looked up to the ceiling thinking. "Why do you think that is?" he said.

"I'm not sure," Megan replied. "But it seems that many of these programs could be solutions looking for a problem."

"I'm not sure about that. It could be that people don't know how to access the resources or that the details of the program have too many strings attached or maybe the programs aren't very well run," Will commented.

"What about the contracting and supplier diversity programs? You said they had better participation?" Max asked.

"Yes, they do, at least participation to the level of getting certified and getting their company on the minority business list. But it breaks down after that. Very few of the people on the list ever get any business. And even fewer get any significant business. And it's the same people getting the business year after year," Megan concluded.

"The picture is getting clearer now," Will suggested as he leaned up in his chair. "Now I'm starting to understand some of the frustration and skepticism we heard during our interviews. Picture this: People hear about these programs and they expect that they have a chance to participate."

"Yeah, then they get their company on the list and get no business. They don't really know why but they start to perceive and then believe that organizations are not serious about supplier diversity," added Dionne.

"The general public hears about these programs and the dollars associated and they think minorities are getting rich. Corporations are just as frustrated because they feel as though they are putting the programs together and are not getting any credit for trying," Megan added.

"It doesn't make for a very good environment for minority business development, does it?" Max asked. "The idea of skepticism, is that what we got in the interviews?"

"For the most part, yes," Will answered. "People really don't think anything is going to change. The general feeling is that minority businesses only want a handout and corporations really don't care about minorities."

"I did hear some good rhetoric though. I would call it pessimistically hopeful. People know we have to get this right.

They realize the demographic shifts behind the idea of inclusion. Their words indicate they understand the potential benefits but at a heart level I'm just not sure they *believe* it can happen," Megan added.

"I did hear some other recurring themes that seem important," Will said. "The interviewees on all sides of this issue also talked about the importance of a business owner having real and actionable relationships. These are relationships with people who are both willing and able to *hook you up.* "

The group smiled listening to Will.

He continued, "The other theme I heard from various categories of people was the idea that the minority business had to be ready to do business and be focused on the needs of the customer. I had to fight not to let this one get to me."

"Why would that get to you?" Megan asked.

"Because I'm not sure I'm willing to concede that minorities are not ready to do business. The generalization feels too big," Will responded.

"I'm not sure that's what the interviewees were saying," Megan said. "I heard the same thing and my perception was that they meant that minority business capacity and experience doing business with corporations was limited."

"See, I heard it a different way," Dionne interrupted. "I think all of these programs and the promotion of the programs have changed the natural dynamics of business. What I thought I heard was that minorities come to the corporations expecting an opportunity. The corporations want them to come looking to provide added value products and services that help the corporation be more successful."

"I think we all might be saying variations on the same thing. We can't forget or avoid the fact that there are fundamentals of business. The basis of all business is the same no matter what the race or gender of the business owner. Business is an exchange of value. You have what I want, money. I have what you want, a product or service. That's business," Max concluded as he stood and moved toward the flip chart stand in the corner of the room.

"The big question now is, what is all of this telling us? What are the few realities that matter the most to our mission of accelerating the growth of minority businesses?" Max asked, looking at the group for answers.

The group was quiet. Max just waited.

Dionne spoke first, "One of the first realities is that minority businesses are too small and too often in non-strategic businesses."

Max wrote Dionne's point on the flip chart.

Will was next. "It is a reality that minority business owners are less likely to have actionable relationships. Their entrepreneurial networks for flushing out ideas, getting capital, finding strategic opportunities, giving input on deal structure, and general guidance are limiting."

"The simple measures of success are also a reality," Megan added. "We haven't talked about it yet, but the primary measure of success if you are a government agency is the percent of dollars spent with minority firms. For major corporations it's the total dollar amount spent. And although I know the numbers are easy to communicate, they really don't measure progress. This may have been the approach that brought us to this point, but I think we need some additional measures if we plan to accelerate our progress."

"That is an interesting point," Max said writing it on the flip chart. "There is no doubt that the way we measure success might have a lot to do with our methods of achieving success. Are there any other realities?"

"Well, I would suggest that we cannot ignore the current environment for inclusion. Things like the tone of our public and private conversations, the level of authentic dialogue about the real issues, and the level of leadership engagement around this issue all lead to a tough environment in which to make any new ideas about minority business work. If anything is really going to happen, we will have to improve the environment for inclusion in The City," Will added.

"I agree. And with the amount of skepticism we have been hearing, that change will not be easy." Max paused and looked around the table. "Does anyone have anything else?" He put the marker away and sat down and reviewed the notes on the flip chart. "Our four realities: 1.Often too small and non-strategic, 2. Less likely to have actionable entrepreneurial networks, 3. The measures of success are simplistic, and 4. The environment for inclusion is strained."

"What is our next step, Max?" Megan asked.

"Our next step is to spend the next month with these four realities. Think about them and their implications. Begin to discuss together how we can positively affect these four realities. We'll meet here next week at the same time. Everyone cool?" Max asked.

Everyone nodded. "Thank you all for your time today. This is good stuff."

The group slowly gathered their things. They talked and joked with each other as they left. Max sat silently in the Mount Union conference room. For the next two hours he looked through his notes and reviewed the many flip charts the group had created. He felt good about the progress the team had made. He was comfortable with the type and quality of the data that was presented.

Two things bothered him; first, he was not sure they could turn this into success for minority businesses; second, he knew none of this was going to work without people working with it. *We have to find a way to deal with the skepticism. I need help on this one*, he thought. He leaned forward, grabbed the conference room telephone and dialed. "Hugh, this is Max. You have a minute to get together?"

CHAPTER
9

SUCCESS AND
SKEPTICISM

The Country Club was only a few blocks away. Max was relieved that Hugh had time to meet with him. He had so many thoughts going through his head. He was 45 years old and by almost every account he was living the American Dream. His valve manufacturing business had grown well. The decision to sell his company was a tough one but the financial gain was too significant to let pass. He was financially set. He had been married to Dawn for 20 years. He always said she was the real reason for his success. They had two great kids. Sidney, their daughter, was a sophomore at Agnes Scott College in Atlanta, Georgia, and their son Mitchell was a freshman at Howard University in Washington D.C. Life was pretty good. *But how did it happen?* Max thought.

He turned into a parking space and got out of the car. He unbuttoned the cuffs on his shirt and rolled up his sleeves as he walked into the club. Hugh was waiting at the observation window watching two young boys play tennis.

"They're pretty good, aren't they?" Hugh said.

"They are good. They look like they're in high school. How old do they look to you?" Max asked.

"Max, when you get to my age they all look pretty young." The men both smiled. "This is an interesting moment," Hugh continued.

"What do you mean?"

"I mean here we are, two black men, at a private country club and we're not working," Hugh said with subtle grin. "You are one of the most successful entrepreneurs in the The City. We are watching a white kid and a black kid play competitive tennis. It wasn't long ago that this moment was just not possible."

"You know, Hugh, that's part of what I want to talk to you about. I'm not sure how this all happens. I've done pretty well in business. I lived the experience and I'm still not sure exactly what made it work. When I hear the frustration from other minorities, I feel it with them but my experience has been so different. I've been frustrated with the system but not like that," Max explained.

"Are you asking how success happens?" Hugh said looking straight at Max.

"Yes, I guess I am."

"Well call your wife and tell her you'll be home for dinner because this will be a short meeting. The answer to your question is, I don't know," Hugh said refocusing his eyes on the tennis match.

"Come on, Hugh. You know what I'm asking."

"Max, you cannot make success happen for someone. No goal, no set-aside, no program can create success. Think about this; have you ever heard of a bank financing program that lowered the requirements for minority businesses?"

"Sure I have," Max replied.

"It would work great if all they needed was money. Have you ever heard of government set-aside programs that demand certain amounts of work be done by minority firms?"

Max nodded.

"That would be perfect if all they needed was more business. The point is that success is different for everyone and it's never guaranteed."

Hugh pointed to the tennis court. "Max, how are those two boys able to be competitive with each other?"

"What do you mean?"

"Does one of them have a larger racket? Better gym shoes? Does one of them have a closer relationship with the line judge?" Hugh asked smiling.

Max smiled too.

"Look over there. See that couple and that one over there?" Hugh said pointing to the other side of the room. "Those are the two boys' parents. Now watch the way the boys strike the ball. They both have talent. They understand the game. Observe the way they come to the net. They want to compete and they expect to win."

The two men just watched for a while. Hugh broke the silence. "Max, those are the elements that make them competitive."

"Man, Hugh, I hate when you do that. I hate when you give me these puzzles."

Hugh smiled again. "It's not a puzzle, Max. I wouldn't do that to you. This is an example of how success happens. It takes all of the things we just talked about. Those boys can compete because they have had exposure and they have been supported. They have real talent but they also understand the game. They've been coached, meaning someone has told them the truth about their play and how to improve. They have clearly worked hard to be good, but they also have a strong desire to pursue winning."

"Some of it they got from their parents, some from coaches, some of it they got from God, and the rest they had to want for themselves," Max added.

"You got it, Max, I know it sounds corny but the old adage is true, 'success is where opportunity meets preparation.'"

Hugh moved closer to Max and pointed. "Just like those boys' parents, we can't create success. The best we can do is to attempt to increase the likelihood they can compete. Things are never equal, Max. One of these boys may have to play with the wind in their face for an entire match or with a slight injury."

Max nodded his head in agreement. "And dealing with all of that just becomes a part of what it takes to be successful."

"Exactly. Your job is to help with the ingredients of success you can, and help the people who have the other ingredients that are needed," Hugh concluded.

"I got it. Now all I have to do is to get people to give any of this a chance," Max said.

"Will that be a problem?"

"Hugh, no one *believes* anything will change. The more they already know about supplier diversity, the more skeptical they are."

"Well, why should they believe, Max? The stereotypes always lead us back to what we already thought was true. People think what they think."

"How can we hope to ever get anything to change if no one is willing to try?" Max asked.

"Max, I'm surprised that you're surprised by the response you're getting. Why do *you* believe something can change?"

"Because I've seen it happen. I've lived the experience. I know things can work," Max replied.

"Have the people you think are so skeptical seen it work? Have they lived the experience? What others have seen is less than success in their minds. They have heard promises that haven't been kept. They have given effort and seen people not take advantage of it. If you want a new reality, then you must make a new reality. Non-believers will believe only when they see results over and over again," Hugh insisted.

"It's going to be difficult to make progress in an environment of such skepticism."

"Max, don't try to convert the non-believers. You can't focus on those minorities that don't want to believe anything will ever change. Whites that think we have already given minorities too much also can't be your focus. You will spend too much time and too much energy, and without results their thinking still won't change anyway. Focus on those folks who at least want to believe. Focus on the people who are open to giving things a chance. Find the people who have the most to gain and who are most prepared to take advantage of progress. Catch the others later," Hugh advised.

"All of that wisdom, and we never even sat down," Max said.

Hugh just shrugged his shoulders "Get out of here. I want to finish watching my great grandson's tennis match."

Max just shook his head. "Your great grandson." He smiled patting Hugh on the back. "I'll talk to you later."

Hugh threw up his hand to say goodbye, "Remember, you convert skeptics one new reality at a time. Your job is to create a great plan. You will never convince everyone."

"I got it. Thanks," Max said as he walked away. *Hugh is right.* Max thought. *We can't guarantee success but we can certainly build a better infrastructure for it. And although we have a lot of skeptics, we have to focus on those who are ready to believe.*

"They'll be trying to make it look like something they already know and then condemn it as being business as usual."

CHAPTER
10

WHAT'S THE PLAN?

Max came downstairs buttoning the last button on his shirt cuff. His wife, Dawn, handed him a cup of coffee.

"Thanks, baby."

"No problem, Maxwell. I know you have a lot on your mind," she said with the innocent smile she liked to use on him. "I haven't seen you this fired up since you started your business."

Max had not noticed being *fired up*, but he did feel emotionally connected to this effort. It felt special. It felt like it mattered. It felt like it could really make a difference. God knows it had occupied his time. He had spent the last month going over his notes again and again. He talked to even more business owners, corporate executives and community activists. He wanted to be sure he really understood what all of the information meant. He was ready for the team's solution development meetings that were starting today.

Max looked at Dawn and smiled. He could never forget how important her support had always been.

"I have to get going," Max said as he bent over to kiss her goodbye. He grabbed his briefcase and overcoat and headed for the door.

He arrived at the office building 15 minutes early. He entered the Mount Union Conference room and put down his things. The walls were covered with flip chart paper and the signs Kalm had made. It was beginning to look like a war room.

The others entered the room one-by-one. The group had really come together over the last few months. Everyone seemed to really enjoy the company of the others and value their diverse perspectives.

"Well, I hope you brought your sleeping bags," Max said smiling. "We have a lot of work to do over the next few weeks. I expect that the days will be long. We have catered breakfast, lunch and dinner. We want you to be comfortable, so if you need anything, just ask. Megan has shared with me a process for solution development that we both think will move us along and end with a set of solutions that we can use."

"I would have been shocked if she hadn't," Will joked.

Megan smiled and the others laughed. She was really process oriented. "OK, so you guys are starting to know me. Anyway, I was thinking that we start with the four realities that were the outcomes of our research. Of all of the things we reviewed, these were the items that we determined mattered the most. It seems to make sense that our solutions should seek to accelerate progress with these four realities. We take one reality at a time and devise strategies to address it. Once we're finished, we check our solutions to see how they work together."

"I'm cool with the approach. Just remember," Max said pointing to one of the posters, "focus, make it doable, make it new, make it sustainable and don't crush history. Is everyone ready to get to work?"

Everyone nodded.

"Great! Let's do it! It might be good to start by reviewing the four realties....."

Kalm moved to the wall where the four realities were written. She began to read them. Max leaned back in his seat. His mind was wandering with thoughts of everything they had done in such a short period of time. All of that effort has been for what they were about to do next. He leaned back up in his seat and gave Kalm his full attention.

*   *   *   *   *

The team meetings had all gone late into the evening. The Mount Union conference room was beginning to look like a college fraternity house. There were markers and large pieces of paper everywhere. There were Chinese food cartons and soda pop cans on the conference table and balls of abandoned paper on the floor. It was week three and they had debated, presented and discussed many different elements of their plan. They were all exhausted but extremely excited about what the plan was proposing.

"That's it," Max said putting the cap back on the marker. "I think we're ready. What do you think?"

"Oh, I think *we're* ready. The question is, are they ready for us?" Will said.

"You're right. With our current environment people will be skeptical about any of this working," Megan added.

"They'll be trying to make it look like something they already know and then condemn it as being business as usual," Kalm added.

"Wow, talk about skeptical, you're leading the pack. Our job was to develop a plan that would work. We will never convince *everyone* that this or any other solution is a good idea. We are looking for those who are willing to try. Everyone is not going to get it. We can't waste our time, energy and emotions on trying to bring everyone along. We have done very good work here. We have to *believe* that it is going to make a difference."

Max looked at his watch. "It's getting late. We could all probably use some rest. I'll arrange the presentation time and get back to all of you. I hope you feel as good about the work we did here as I do. Thanks again for agreeing to work this hard."

"Well I'm not sure we ever agreed to work this hard but it was our pleasure, Max. Thanks for letting us go along for the ride," Megan said.

The others nodded as they collected their things to leave.

After a few moments Max was alone in the Mount Union conference room. He took one more glance around the room. *We really got to the truth about the issues of business and race,* he thought. *I wonder if people will be able to suspend their own notions long enough to consider how this all might work.* He pulled out his cell phone and dialed Don Dressel's home telephone number.

"Don, Max Albert. Sorry to call you so late, but I thought you'd like to know that we're ready."

"I'll call the CEOs together," Don said.

"Don, let's start modeling a different approach. Let's make sure that we invite minority CEOs and others with a vested interest in minority business development. This is a great chance for us to have an authentic conversation about the issues."

"Great idea, Max."

"Great. Kalm will get you a list of suggested attendees and you can take it from there."

"No problem. Max, is it good?"

"Don, it'll work and we can't wait to show it to you."

"These are the entrepreneurs that will generate the type of impact that we all want from this effort."

CHAPTER 11

BUILDING CAPACITY
IN THE SWEET SPOT

D
on Dressel was completing his introduction of Max
and the rest of the team. There were about 40
people present. The group was quite diverse. There
were the corporate CEOs that originally approached Max to
consider this project. There were minority CEOs who had
been a part of the interviewing process. There were corporate
supplier diversity directors who had lent their expertise along
the way. There was representation from every Chamber of
Commerce in the area, including the Hispanic and African
American Chambers. There were minority business advocates,
including The City Minority Supplier Business Council and
the Minority Business Incubator. Max had also asked his friend
Miguel to attend the meeting to hear about the plan first hand.

"Thanks, Don, and thank you all for coming," Max said as he
rose from his seat and moved to the front of the small audito-
rium. "We have put a lot of hours into this project. Many of
you have helped us with information, insight and encourage-

ment. We appreciate all that you've done to get us to this point. What we found in our research was that we are making efforts to progress in diversifying the supplier base. Corporate spending with minority suppliers is on the rise. Attention on this topic has increased. But although positive efforts exist, progress is not keeping pace with the rate of change in our racial demographics. What blocks us most from true breakthroughs in minority economic inclusion is a lack of considerable capacity, particularly strategic capacity," Max explained.

"Under our current model, minority businesses are generally too small and there are too few exceptions to that rule. The corporations are therefore squeezed between goals of increased minority spending and few minority businesses with significant capacity."

"The outcome is that corporations do considerable work with very few minority suppliers. They do small transactions of ancillary work with a slightly larger group of minority businesses," Max continued.

"There is nothing wrong with these smaller transactions. They are needed services that drive revenue and provide access for minority firms to potentially valuable corporate relationships. But they are not strategic, or vital to the success of the major corporation. Vendors are not linked to the primary demand of the corporation's customer."

"In the past no one has cared what type of business it was as long as it's business. What we are suggesting is that we should all care. The goal should be that minority businesses have more capacity and are more able to compete, not just that they did more business. Part of the reason minority businesses lack capacity is because of the type of businesses they are in. Services like janitorial, office supplies, security, training and even facilities engineering are businesses with low barriers to entry, but their opportunity is too often commodity driven, low profit, low value add and easily replaceable."

"So capacity building is the back drop of our presentation. If we agree that capacity is important and that adding value to corporations matters, then we should all care what type of business we are doing. This does not mean we don't keep doing what we're doing and making the progress we're making. This isn't an 'either or.' We hope it's 'and both.' The point is that capacity matters and the question is how do we grow capacity?"

Max moved to his left and picked up the remote control to the projector. "Our team nicknamed this project 'The Accelerator' because of the repeated request from the community to accelerate the pace of progress. The agenda for today's presentation is as follows: first we will talk about the *mission* of this initiative. We will discuss what The Accelerator will be — basically its *form*. We will spend some time talking about the *target market* and then some new ideas about how we *measure success*. We will share information about the *primary roles* of The Accelerator and we will conclude our presentation by describing the *staff skills* we think are vital to have in The Accelerator."

He pushed the button on the remote and advanced to the next slide.

85

"Ladies and gentlemen, our mission is to increase the *number* of sizable minority businesses. We must not forget the reason this team was brought together in the first place. This started out about improving our community for everyone. The thought at the time was that more sizable minority businesses would mean better minority employment, an increased tax base, improved neighborhoods and better schools. The premise was that everyone would win with an increased number of sizable minority businesses. Corporations would have better and more diverse suppliers, the community would be more attractive for outside investment and as a place to live, work and play. Our research on the employment patterns of minority entrepreneurs and the purchasing patterns of major corporations gave our team real evidence that suggest that this mission is the right one."

Max cleared his throat and advanced the projector to the next slide.

"So what is the Accelerator? Well, it will be a small, nimble entrepreneurial organization. The Accelerator will function much like a venture capital firm, with one very big exception."

Max paused.

"They'll have no capital to invest." The group laughed. "Seriously, we use the venture capital firm as an analogy to indicate the depth of involvement of the Accelerator. Many people don't realize the money is typically a very small part of the type of assistance a venture capital firm provides. This chart shows you the roles of the Accelerator and compares them to the roles of a venture capital firm. It's key that this

The Accelerator Similarity to Venture Capital Firm

Role	Venture Capital	The Accelerator
Portfolio of Companies	✓	✓
Relationships to funding sources	✓	✓
Assist w/access to markets	✓	✓
Facilitator of technical assistance	✓	✓
Seeking firms that can grow	✓	✓
Minority focus, sensitivity, access, credibility, etc.	✓ ?	✓
Source of capital	✓	N/A

organization have relationships and credibility with funding sources, major corporations and minority business owners. The Accelerator must know these groups and understand their strengths and weaknesses and what they are looking for in businesses that they do business with. Many of these groups don't believe in one another right now and The Accelerator's overriding mission is to help them believe. We will talk more about this idea of credibility later."

Max put up the next slide. "The Accelerator will have a "portfolio" of minority businesses that meet the criteria of being ready to accelerate. This is our *target market*. Our team struggled with what were the right criteria but the data lead us to the following criteria to use, at least as a starting point. The firms in the portfolio should be $1 million or larger in sales. They should have three plus years of experience and be in an industry that can attract capital. These are criteria but there will obviously be exceptions. What is most important is that they are accelerate-able. The real driver behind what types of minority businesses will be in the portfolio will be the market demand and, to some extent, the type of minority businesses and management expertise that currently exist. A sort of blending of what we have, and what major corporations and organizations need."

Max put down the remote control and turned to face the audience.

"While $1 million firms may not sound very large to some, we decided to set the threshold there for two reasons. First, based on the data we collected, we have very few minority businesses over $1 million. We were almost forced to start there in order to have some critical mass. The second reason is that we really believe this is the sweet spot for the Accelerator to really make a difference," Max explained.

"Think of minority business theoretically in three different dimensions. The first dimension doesn't know or even care what we are talking about today. These are what we would call 'mom and pop' businesses. Because of the experience and aspirations of the owners and the nature of their business, this level of business is designed to remain small."

"Let me skip to the third dimension," Max suggested. "In this dimension the businesses and entrepreneurs are more sophisticated. They are often involved in large complex transactions. Based on the experience, resources and connections of the owners in this dimension, these deals are likely already in the market flow. The Accelerator will have very little impact on whether they happen or not. The value the Accelerator is designed to add, these businesses already have. The best we could do is to go along for the ride and seek to share the credit for the success. That is more window dressing than real value added. Also the number of deals in the third dimension is very low. We think it is important to do a volume of deals, and third dimension deals just don't come along often."

"I'm also saying that if we only pursue opportunities in the third dimension we will create very little noticeable change. It will still be the same connected people getting the deals done."

Max was gauging the response from the audience. People were clearly trying to get their hands around this idea.

Max continued. "That brings us back to the second dimension of minority businesses. In this dimension the business owner has a solid track record either in business or as business managers inside of a major corporation. They know what they are doing. Many have been in business for awhile but generally have $1 million - $10 million dollars in sales. These are the minority entrepreneurs you see and count on in The City, or the corporate managers that have had solid careers. They don't have major entrepreneurial connections and although they are capable they have not been exposed to highly complex business transactions. These are the entrepreneurs who hire more minorities and give to local causes. These are the entrepreneurs that will generate the type of impact that we all want from this effort. And maybe most important of all, these are the businesses The Accelerator can really affect. This is our *sweet spot*. Just like any other business, The Accelerator must find the space where it can add the most value. The second dimension is it. The number of businesses in this dimension, the experience and visibility of the owners of these businesses, and their proven commitment to our community make them great investments of our attention."

Max reached down to the table to adjust some papers and then advanced to the next slide.

"Before we begin to talk about the primary roles of The Accelerator I want to take a few minutes to discuss how we measure success. We, as a community, have been working so hard on making progress that I think we have gotten the goals confused with the measures," Max offered.

Three Dimensions of Minority Business			
	1st Dimension Mom & Pop	**2nd** Dimension Willing, able	**3rd** Dimension Well connected, exposed, complex
Growth Orientation	Limited	Moderate to Significant	Significant
Bank Ability & Resources	Limited	Adequate	Adequate
Business Experience or Sophistication	Limited to Moderate	Moderate to Significant	Significant
Actionable Relationships	Limited	Limited to Moderate	Significant

"It seems that the goal has become to increase the level of spending by corporations exemplified by awards like the Billion Dollar Club, an elite group of major corporations that spend at least $1 billion with minority suppliers. Everyone is focused on the spending. But that is a measure, not the goal. The reason for all of this is to increase the economic inclusion of minorities and to provide real opportunities for success. Tracking the spending is not a bad thing as long as we don't get lulled into the belief that spending alone equals economic inclusion.

"The spending numbers are easy to track and communicate. They are a clear way to demonstrate corporate commitment and to compare a corporation to others. But the spending goals may not translate to the achievement of the real purpose of supplier diversity programs. The numbers we should really be paying attention to are how many businesses in the second dimension went from $3 million to $10 million and from $10 million to $20 million. This is the type of tangible progress that will increase minority inclusion. This is the type of progress that everyday people can see and understand. This is the type of progress that inspires more entrepreneurship."

"Max, OK. I understand the goal," said John Stevens, the CEO of Venture Steel. "I set the vision for our desire to increase the amount of business we do with minority suppliers. Based on what I'm coming to understand from the work you have done, I admit I can raise the priority of this issue to a higher level inside our company. But we do already have a supplier diversity program in place. We attend the right events and we even make our efforts in this area a part of our managers' evaluation. The people at the operations level of my company tell me that they can't find minority venders that are ready. They tell me that to increase our spending with minority businesses at any faster rate would mean a tradeoff on quality."

The minorities in the room were clearly bothered by John's comments. Miguel was calm but clearly wanted to respond. Max paused for a moment.

"You know John, we heard that exact comment during our interviews with corporate representatives across lines of race, industry and company size. The common responses to your question are that you haven't tried hard enough," Max explained using his fingers to count his comments. "You don't know where to look. You need a better program with more aggressive goals. You have processes in your procurement system that make it difficult for minorities to participate."

Max put down the remote control and walked around the table from which he was presenting.

"And although it makes sense to examine all of those potential solutions, our research suggests that it is not quite that simple. This is a touchy subject and I know my comments might be taken wrong or used to justify someone's already tainted views but it's just time to be real. We can not keep dancing around this issue. The truth is that too few minority businesses are ready to do the types of strategic business that we are talking about here. But we have to take this in some type of context. The reality is, most businesses of any race aren't ready. Most don't have the capacity, experience or the expertise to do strategic business with a major corporation."

Max's conversation with Hugh came into his mind.

"The plan that we are presenting to you today is designed to challenge your thinking at another level. When people say 'minority businesses aren't ready,' in some cases they're right. People who haven't done it often don't know how. The problem is that we have been saying 'they aren't ready' so long that we might be looking for their shortcomings versus their potential. There is a significant difference between the business not being ready and the business owner not being ready. We think business owners in the second dimension we discussed earlier are ready. The mission of The Accelerator is to help their businesses become more ready to do business with you."

John just nodded. Max continued.

"We know that to be competitive you need a vibrant market of consumers and a solid core of quality suppliers. Our research suggests that to do either long-term will require a strong minority business environment. Let us finish the presentation and I think you will see how we can really address these issues in such a way that everyone wins."

CHAPTER
12

ACCELERATING ENTREPRENEURIAL NETWORKS

M ax pushed the button on the remote control and advanced the next slide.

"To review, our goal is to build capacity. The target audience is what we have defined as minority firms in the second dimension," Max reviewed. "And we used the venture capital firm analogy to illustrate the level of involvement of The Accelerator. This is a perfect lead into the primary roles of The Accelerator. Simply stated, the success of The Accelerator rests on the strength of its entrepreneurial network, and accelerating the entrepreneurial networks of minority firms is a primary role," Max explained.

"As we evaluated the success stories of those second dimension minority entrepreneurs that became suppliers in a significant way, they all talked about these actionable relationships, or what we are calling entrepreneurial networks. The idea is supported in repeated research, and it just makes sense. The strength, depth and breadth of one's entrepreneurial network is directly related to the level of any business's success."

The group just listened.

"Then we did a non-scientific comparison of entrepreneurial networks," Max said smiling. "What we realized was that who you show your idea to contributes a lot to how well thought through your idea becomes. Who you show your idea to helps you realize what is possible and helps you formulate the most effective process and the resources required to move your idea forward. The minority entrepreneur's network has fewer complex business experiences, fewer significant resources and a limited network of their own. Even if they want to help, their ability to do so is limited."

"That's enlightening," Don said nodding his head.

"I agree. That is enlightening. Tell me Max, why not make The Accelerator an actual venture capital firm?" asked Rob Mindel, the CEO of VanHunt Financial.

"That's a good question. We considered it, but we don't think that approach will work. The effort of putting a fund together is significant, and our research did not find minority focused funds to be a best practice. It also would shift our focus to fund development and away from our core mission. We also think it fails to address the problem. The problem is that minority businesses are not in the main stream deal flow. If a business deal is a good deal for a minority focused venture fund, why wouldn't it be a good deal for any fund? A good deal is a good deal. We need to create more good deals. If we run into problems getting venture firms and other capital sources to seriously consider minority businesses, we can always consider adding fund development later. Keep in mind that overcoming the traditional concerns about funding is exactly the role of The Accelerator."

"Max, I'm still not sure I see the venture capital firm analogy," the president of the local incubator remarked.

The question caught Max taking a drink from his bottle of water.

"This is a difficult idea to explain," Max conceded. "What we found in our research is that businesses that are *accepted* into a venture capital firm's portfolio get much more attention and resources than just money. The venture capital firm sees their potential, but it is also very involved with improving the readiness of the business. For example, they may connect the firm with an operations expert to improve a lagging piece of their business. They may give them advice to restructure their financials to be more ready for future investments from other investors. Venture capitalists often fund part of the deal, but refer the company to other capital sources for additional funding. In many cases the venture capital firm has connections with major corporations who could become customers of the firms in their portfolio. The Accelerator will do all of those things."

"How far do you plan to go with this? How involved will The Accelerator be?" Don Dressel asked.

"We plan to go all the way," Max responded. "If an entrepreneur that meets the criteria to be in our portfolio has a business plan that is lacking, we are going to tell them that it's lacking and hook them up with someone that can help them make it better. If they don't understand how to put together a merger or acquisition, we are going to help them. Study after study suggests that the entrepreneur's network is vital to their success."

"And The Accelerator is going to be their network?" Don asked.

"Well, I don't want to assume that these entrepreneurs don't already have a solid network. What we want to do is extend their network to the level that accelerates their business growth, just like a venture capital firm. If we are going to allow these companies to trade on our reputation, The Accelerator must know everything about them. Portfolio companies will be expected to disclose details about their financials, their operations, their customer base, about everything."

"That seems like you will be too involved," one of the Black CEOs commented.

"Our preliminary conversations with minority business owners suggest that you may be right. Many will think this is too much. We believe they think this way for two reasons. First, because they don't *believe* it will make any difference. Most minority business owners are sick of filling out special paperwork, submitting personal financial information and attending special 'How-to-do-business-with' conferences and getting no real benefit. The second reason business owners may not want The Accelerator this involved is because they do not trust the confidentiality of the organization."

Max put the remote control down again.

"These are real and significant considerations but they are challenges that can be overcome. This is no different from working with a bank or venture capital firm. If you want their capital, this is what it takes. The mission of The Accelerator is to know what it takes and to have the relationships to connect the firms that are ready. We believe to do this effectively means that The Accelerator must *know* the businesses in their portfolio. If not, they are nothing more than a referral agency and we are back where we started. The Accelerator must earn the right to ask for the amount of data they want and they will do that by giving business owners a real reason to *believe* The Accelerator will make a difference," Max explained.

"Trust me, I know what you're talking about," Max continued addressing this concern. "I've done what you do. I've been to the conferences; I've filled out the paperwork. I've felt what you feel. There are many reasons why all of these hoops exist. Some are necessary to fulfill the mission and others are in place to grease the gears of a bureaucratic system. The Accelerator needs this level of information to leverage their entrepreneurial network on your behalf."

Max thought about trying to continue to explain how important this information is but he remembered what Hugh had said about dealing with skepticism. *Go with those who are ready.* Max decided to move on. He advanced to the next slide.

"We have been focused on the minority businesses. But the success of The Accelerator is also dependent on a fresh engagement by major corporations. Many major corporations and other organizations already have supplier diversity programs or some level of focus on doing business with a diverse population of firms. Our research suggested that even organizations that don't have formal programs in place have a real interest in the issue."

"Max, for those corporations that do not have programs but want to, will The Accelerator help companies create effective programs?" asked Bob Grum, CEO of The City Power and Light.

"Bob, the short answer is no. There are consultants and other organizations that do that type of thing as their core business."

"To be candid, we have worked with some of those groups and many are not very good," Bob continued.

"I understand," Max sighed. "Our team discussed this issue a lot. What we found was that there were a number of areas related to minority business development that needed improvement. For example, we couldn't find an accurate database of minority-owned businesses. It's dangerous to attempt to use the Accelerator to fix everything that's not working. We decided that the best approach for the Accelerator is to stay focused on the narrow mission."

"Nice idea, but how do these other things get fixed?" Bob probed.

"I'm not sure I have the complete answer, but I know nothing good happens if we keep funding organizations that aren't working. It may be politically correct but it isn't helping anyone. We can't keep mistaking flapping our wings with actually flying. And flapping our wings faster only creates more wind."

Bob smiled and nodded his head, indicating he understood. Max looked at his watch.

"We have been at it for over an hour. This feels like a good place to take a break. When we come back we will talk about the corporations' role in The Accelerator and the Accelerator Relationships. See you all in 10 minutes."

"...improve the readiness of minority businesses and bridge the gap in relationships..."

13

ACCELERATOR RELATIONSHIPS

M ost of the group was back in the room. Max motioned to Don Dressell to come to the front.

"I noticed that a few people left. What happened?" Max asked.

"It appears that they didn't like the way you addressed some issues. They didn't like how you addressed the issue of minorities not being ready," Don replied.

"What didn't they like?" Max whispered.

"Some minorities thought you admitted they weren't ready and the corporate representatives felt you were making excuses and blaming the problem on them. And some of the minority business development organizations thought you were being too critical of them too."

"I was afraid that would happen. It's hard to get people to really listen to your whole idea when there is so much emotion involved in the topic," Max explained.

"Max, don't worry about it. I didn't hear you saying any of those things. I think you are right on point. We just have to go with the ones that are ready."

Don turned away to address the audience.

"Ladies and gentlemen, Max is about to get going again," Don said.

People quickly ended conversations and began to take their seats.

"During our research…," Max said advancing the projector to the next slide. "…we evaluated the relationship between corporations and their strategic suppliers. We wanted to understand how these suppliers who were critical to the success of the corporation worked with the corporations. I'm talking about strategic supplier relationships irrespective of race. What we found was that these were long term relationships that had a significant level of investment from both the supplier and the corporation. These became our *model* relationships and the type we seek to simulate with The Accelerator. Of course every corporation's approach was different but there were a number of things they had in common. For example, they often offered their strategic suppliers engineering expertise, operations consultation and executive level relationships. What we found was that they offered whatever they believed it would take to make a good supplier a great strategic supplier. These are relationships that our team started calling Accelerator Relationships. We're suggesting that this is the model for how corporations who agree to participate with The Accelerator will approach minority suppliers in The Accelerator portfolio."

Max moved to the next slide.

"One of the obvious challenges is that many major corporations are trying to reduce their costs and their number of direct suppliers. It is important that I make two points. First, this is not a request to provide more resources. We have found that this is fundamentally how corporations do strategic sourcing today. We are proposing that corporations extend that approach to minority suppliers who they believe have the basic tenets to become strategic partners."

Using his fingers to count, Max continued, "Second, every major corporation will implement this idea in their own way. It will have to fit how their corporation does business. Keep in mind, this model works just the same with your tier one or direct suppliers that may work with minority suppliers at the tier two level. The leadership and expectations still come from your corporation. You'll probably need to help tier one suppliers understand how important doing *strategic* sourcing with minority suppliers is to your corporation. The bottom line to making this successful is that everyone has to understand that your corporation is committed to minority business acceleration."

"Max, can you give us an example of how this might work?" Bob asked.

"Sure. I'll give you a scenario for how the entire accelerator process might work in a practical case. Let's say that you're a consumer products company and you need warehousing and logistics capacity. There is a minority business in your community that performs that service but, like other suppliers that have not done business with you before they don't know how to do things your way. The Accelerator will work with the minority business. If they have the management capacity and expertise to grow, then The Accelerator will help position them to be attractive to capital sources. They will also position them to be a strategic supplier with your corporation. And that is where the Accelerator Relationships come in. Your corporation works with the minority supplier to help them understand your requirements and put the right systems in place to add value to your business. For example, they may need to align their electronic data interchange systems with yours; or they may need exposure to your particular quality measurement systems or software upgrades for logistics systems. The key is that you need additional warehousing and logistics capacity anyway. You were going to work with some vendor to meet your needs. You now have diversified your supplier base and you have a new relationship with a strategic supplier who is more ready to compete for your future business. The big point here is that none of this is different from what most major corporations do as a matter of routine. By the way, the opportunity to do business with your corporation may make the minority business even more attractive to capital sources, which further increases their capacity to serve you and other customers."

"Max, I want to make sure I understand how the various pieces of this fit together. You and your team are saying that

The Accelerator will improve the readiness of minority businesses and bridge the gap in relationships with capital sources and major corporations and organizations that could be potential customers. On the other side, you want corporations to commit to these Accelerator Relationships to increase the opportunity for strategic suppliers."

"Yes, that's pretty much it. And what we found was that almost all minority suppliers who had become strategic suppliers to major corporations had the type of relationship experience just described. We are confident that in the rare cases when minority businesses become strategic suppliers, this is how it works. The Accelerator will help them be more ready and the corporations have to *believe* they can be valuable strategic suppliers."

"What is the role of the corporate Supplier Diversity coordinator in The Accelerator?" asked the representative from The City minority supplier council.

"Their role is essentially the same. They will facilitate introductions to key personnel, they will continue working with tier one suppliers, they will articulate the needs of the corporation and track performance and they will identify minority businesses that may be good candidates for the Accelerator. The big change from what we are doing now is that The Accelerator will deliver more ready minority businesses. The Accelerator is another trusted partner for the Supplier Diversity Coordinator."

Max paused as he watched people gazing at the screen. Some were nodding their heads, others were writing notes. Some were just sitting.

"Keep in mind that the details of this way of doing business are also available in our written report. Many of your detailed questions will be answered there."

"Max, who owns The Accelerator?" asked John Stevens of Venture Steel.

"That is a decision that needs to be made. We are suggesting that a subset of this group act as an advisory board and assume *ownership* of the direction of The Accelerator. The key here is credibility. The Accelerator belongs with a non-profit organization that has significant credibility with corporations, capital sources and 2nd dimension minority business owners. These entities must *believe* that what the chosen organization says is so, and be willing to act based on that belief," Max replied.

"The Accelerator itself will need to be staffed and have some type of infrastructure. Can you give us an idea of the type of skills that will be needed to make The Accelerator successful?" Don asked.

"Yes, there is some level of staffing. You will need an administrative person, but the key position is The Accelerator director. The person that is on point for this initiative must have a successful track record and significant experience with entrepreneurial ventures. You should look for a person who is known and respected by executives of major corporations and people with capital resources. The director must understand minority business and be able to win the confidence of minority business owners. The challenge of the director is to make everyone *believe* this initiative will get results. You need a person with a sense of urgency and passion that will allow The Accelerator to gain momentum. The director will set the tone for how serious everyone is about The Accelerator. It must be immediately obvious that this initiative is different from the local SBA sponsored Small Business Development Center or other programs designed with different missions. I want to ask Megan to come up and spend the next 20 minutes talking about the budget and the implementation plan. Megan."

Max grabbed his bottle of water and took his seat. He didn't hear a word Megan was saying. They were approaching the end. Max was satisfied that they had done a good job presenting the overview. The hard part was ahead, actually implementing and managing the politics.

Don Dressel of The City Bank leaned over and whispered to Max, "Great work. Now we have to figure out how to make this happen."

Miguel caught Max's attention, nodding his head with approval. "Pretty good," he mouthed. "Pretty good." Max just smiled. *I think Miguel wants to believe*, Max thought. They both turned their attention to Megan and her presentation.

"I'm glad you think this thing is worth an investment of your time."

CHAPTER 14

THE CALL TO LEAD
AND TO ACTION

Max was sitting in his office at home reading a newspaper article on The Accelerator. It had been almost two months since he and the team had finished the development work. The City had decided to house the project inside the Chamber of Commerce. Max thought the approach was wise. The response from corporations, minority business owners and the community at large had been mixed, as expected. Most understood the intentions but some didn't *believe* much would happen, but it seemed that there was reason for hope.

"We have raised the funds needed to run The Accelerator," the article read quoting the Chamber Vice President in charge. "We are now in the process of hiring a director to run it."

Max's telephone rang.

"Hello, this is Max Albert."

"Max, this is Miguel."

"Hey, Miguel, what's up?"

"Max, you know that I am on the search committee to find the director for The Accelerator?"

"Yes, I'd heard that. I was just reading the article on The Accelerator in today's paper. I'm glad you think this thing is worth an investment of your time. "

"I know I gave you a hard time about this, Max. The environment had me frustrated and I really let myself become pretty cynical," Miguel said.

"Miguel, I understand. It was never a problem for me. I know you. I know how good you are and how hard you work. I understand how much you love this community. Your comments were more helpful than you might think. You are one of the most even tempered and level-headed thinkers I know. I knew if you were that frustrated that The City was really at a critical crossroad. Your comments helped me know that The Accelerator was worth my time. It was something you helped me understand we had to try," Max explained.

"I'm hoping I can get you to agree again," Miguel said.

"Agree to what?"

"The search committee sent me to talk to you. They, well, we all, think you are the person we need to run The Accelerator," Miguel explained.

"Come on, Miguel. You guys are in the middle of a national search. Give it some time. You're going to get a chance to meet some outstanding talent," Max challenged.

"Max, you've lived it. The people here know you and trust you. You said yourself that credibility was critical to the success of The Accelerator. Plus, think about everything you've learned through the process of putting The Accelerator together. You are the right person," Miguel insisted.

"I'm flattered. But I am not taking this job, Miguel. I'll tell you what I will do. I'll commit a few months to getting The Accelerator up and running. Let's just see what happens after that," Max said.

"That is all we can ask," Miguel replied. "I'll report back to the advisory group."

"That sounds good. You're lucky. You get to talk to the advisory group. I get to tell Dawn I won't be available to perform my extensive list of honey dos."

"Don Dressel? Why would he care about your honey dos?" Miguel asked laughing.

"Dawn, my wife," Max said laughing. "You knew who I meant."

Both men laughed.

"If you'll schedule a meeting for me with the advisory group for next week, I'll put some thoughts and plans together to get us moving," Max said.

"No problem," Miguel replied.

"Great. Get back to me with the date."

"I will. Max, you convinced me we had a chance to do something special. I'm on board now and I look forward to finding new ways for everyone in this community to profit and prosper together," Miguel explained.

"It really is a great opportunity. Let's get it going," Max replied.

"I'll call you back with a date soon."

The two men hung up the telephone. Max turned his office chair around to face the laptop computer on his desk. He retrieved the written Accelerator plan and paged down to the implementation section. For the next few hours Max reviewed the plan, took some notes and began the process of bringing The Accelerator to life.

15

PUSHING ON
THE ACCELERATOR

Max had been running The Accelerator for a little less than four months. The infrastructure was in place and things were beginning to happen. They had begun to build the portfolio of minority firms that were ready for the program. Max had been on a fast paced road show to present The Accelerator, how it works, and the benefits of the initiative. He had visited all of the major corporations and minority business development groups to be sure they understood the mission. They had already seen a few successes. They had helped a minority business owner reassess their value proposition which turned into a new multi-year contract to do packaging for one of the local Fortune 500. They helped a business in The Accelerator portfolio restructure their financials which led to their ability to get additional capital. They had also worked with a small industrial towel manufacturer to retool their business plan which led to a multi-year contract to manufacture private label towels for a major department store chain. The

Accelerator had a sense of momentum that was pushing the organization forward.

"**www.blackwhitegreen.com**," Max mouthed as he typed. He was on-line reviewing the new Accelerator web site which included online information and tools for outside organizations to use. Kalm came into the office.

"It looks good, doesn't it?" she said.

"Yes, it does. More importantly the number of hits we have received is impressive. People are interested in finding out where they are. That's good," Max said.

"Max, there is a Lynn Crew on the telephone. She is the president of the chamber of commerce in Another City. She says she has a few questions for you," Kalm reported.

Max turned his chair around and grabbed the telephone.

"This is Max Albert."

"Max, my name is Lynn Crew and I'm with the chamber of commerce in Another City. I got your name from Don Dressel at The City Bank. We're interested in information about the work you guys did on the Accelerator and Don thought you would be my best source."

"Well Lynn, what do you want to know?" Max asked.

"We've already reviewed the report. I'd like to know what you think we need to know next to get an Accelerator going here in Another City," the lady said.

"Lynn, the first step is finding out who is interested. The trick will be separating those who are really interested from those who show up so that no one thinks they're not interested. We had a slight head start here because people had to invest in the development of The Accelerator plan. We got a pretty good indication of who was really interested because they wrote checks, spent long hours in interviews and things like that," Max explained.

"We've already formed an advisory group to guide our efforts." Lynn replied.

"That sounds perfect. There is nothing more important than making sure that group is diverse and populated with people who can challenge but not be challenging. You need honest and authentic conversations that reflect the reality but don't place blame."

"You said determine who was interested is first. What's next?" Lynn asked.

"The next thing is making sure they really understand the Accelerator idea, how it works, why it is important, and why it is the right, next evolution in business and race," Max responded.

"How did you do that?" Lynn asked.

"We created a presentation that explained it all and we presented it in the key forums in The City. I'll tell you that the presentations went best in the forums that were most diverse. If I were doing it over again I would create the forums and invite key people and groups to them."

"Why is that?" Lynn asked.

"Those types of meetings just worked better. The established group meetings had established group norms and roles and ways of thinking. To communicate The Accelerator you need people's minds to be open to new thinking," Max explained.

"What's next?"

"You go," Max replied. "You've seen the implementation plan. We created a 'Ready List' for minority business owners, major corporations, and community leaders, the three major partners in the success of The Accelerator. The Ready List was a set of questions or statements designed specifically for each group. The goal was to help them begin to position their own efforts to take advantage of the opportunities The Accelerator makes possible."

"Max, would you mind sending me a copy of those three Ready Lists?" Lynn asked.

Max swirled around in his chair to his bookshelf and pulled down a three-ring binder labeled Accelerator Control Book. He paged through a few sections and stopped about a quarter of the way through.

"Sure," Max replied. "I'll fax them right over. You can also get them at our web site **www.blackwhitegreen.com**."

Max paused.

"Lynn, may I give you four pieces of parting advice?" Max asked.

Parting Advice

- Don't let people take you off mission

- Move quickly and gain momentum

- Never fake a success

- Do it before you need to

"Please do. I want to know everything you know," Lynn replied.

"Lynn, my four parting thoughts to you are: 1. Don't let people take you off mission. Stay focused on your target audience and on the value The Accelerator is designed to provide. 2. Move quickly and gain momentum fast. Many people will expect The Accelerator to start to look like others things that, I'm sure, have been tried and failed in Another City. Part of your long-term success will rest in your ability to prove them wrong. 3. Never fake a success. Add real value to real businesses and don't take credit you didn't earn. It might become a habit and if nothing else, it makes people skeptical of why you really exist. 4. Do it before you *need* to. Our community had to have a problem to wake us up. That environment of skepticism, anger and mistrust made everything we had to do more difficult. Whether people think you need an Accelerator or not, start having conversations about economic inclusion." Max concluded.

Lynn thanked Max and they agreed to stay in contact. Max got her fax number and faxed the Ready Lists to her. As he sat down, he began to read them again himself.

Minority Business Owners' Accelerator Ready List

- Do you actively look for opportunities to increase your capacity to provide strategic solutions (not just to do business)?

- Are you focused on adding value to major corporations or on getting an opportunity with them?

- Do you actively seek out and accept advice and guidance?

- Should you be pursuing business with major corporations? Should they be in your target market?

- Are you more competitive today than you were a year ago?

- Is the business you are currently doing with major corporations increasing your firm's capacity to perform? (i.e. Higher bonding, higher certification)

To do:

1. Focus on the value you give to major corporations.

2. Determine the top two or three things that you need to significantly improve your capacity to compete.

Major Corporations'
Accelerator Ready List

• Do your measures of success in supplier diversity reflect the goal of building minority business capacity?

• How many of the dollars spent with minority businesses are spent in strategic sourcing?

• How many current minority suppliers would qualify as strategic suppliers?

• Is your supplier diversity program designed to increase the capacity of minority suppliers or just to increase your level of spending?

To do:

1. Identify good minority suppliers who have the basic elements to become strategic suppliers.

2. Review your goals and measurements to focus them on building capacity

The Community Leaders' Accelerator Ready List

- Does your community engage in frequent and candid conversations about the value of economic inclusion?

- Is economic inclusion a community theme?

- Does your community know the reality of the economic contribution of people of color? (good and bad)

- Does your community have goals and plans for improvement?

To do:

1. Encourage your local paper for a series of articles about topics like shifting racial demographics, the economic opportunity of emerging domestic market, and the impact of a diverse population on recruitment and retention, etc.

2. Frequent mentions about economic inclusion by politicians, CEOs and other community leaders.

3. Support the creation of an Accelerator organization in your community.

Max closed the three-ring binder. He leaned back in his chair and looked out of his office window. It had been a lot of work. Many people in the community had committed their attention, dollars and time to help The Accelerator become a reality. This was not a program pushed by just one segment of our community. *We really did all work together,* he thought. *If we are going to prosper together this will be the way we'll have to work. There really is more profit when we all prosper. We can build better communities and schools and neighborhoods that support the success of all of the people. This is just one example of how. I'm glad we all thought it was important enough.*

What Do I Do Next?

Now what do you do? The short answer is, do something! Start a conversation about economic inclusion. Discuss the barriers. Talk about what is working. Openly discuss what could be better and the frustrations that you have. Listen to the thoughts of others. Use the Accelerator Ready List of questions found in the last chapter to help you get started. Use the context of this book to provide examples and ideas.

We have developed a web site to give you additional tools you can use to determine your evolution and what is next for your organization. Visit our website at **www.blackwhitegreen.com**.

The key message is that economic inclusion is imperative for successful communities and companies. Remember Max's parting advice… "do it before you need to."

ABOUT THE AUTHOR

MELVIN J. GRAVELY II, PH.D.

D r. Gravely is the founder of the Institute for Entrepreneurial Thinking, a for-profit think tank whose mission is to make entrepreneurship more accessible. He has helped thousands of entrepreneurs start and grow their businesses. Mel is also on the business faculty of Thomas More College and is the co-founder of Infrastructure Services, Inc. He writes and speaks on various topics related to entrepreneurial thinking, small business development, and leadership. He is also the author of four other books including *Making It Your Business*, *Grandma's Greatest Gifts* and *The Lost Art of Entrepreneurship*.

He has a BS in computer science from Mount Union College and an MBA from Kent State University. Dr. Gravely's Ph.D. is in Business Administration and Entrepreneurship from The Union Institute. He currently lives in Cincinnati with his family.

Find more information about
Mel Gravely on the web at:
www.melgravely.com

YOUR FEEDBACK PLEASE

If you enjoyed this book you should also read Dr. Gravely's previous book, *The Lost Art of Entrepreneurship*. You will have the chance to encounter wise Hugh again in another story full of practical lessons and solid strategies. The story is quick and entertaining but the proven principles will last a lifetime.

We want to hear from you. What did you think of *When Black and White Make Green*? How did the book affect your business, supplier program or community efforts? Tell us about your success stories discussing and implementing the ideas.

You can email us at:
info@entrethinking.com
or
Mail your comments to:
Institute for Entrepreneurial Thinking
Attn: When Black and White Make Green
P.O. Box 621170
Cincinnati, Ohio 45262-1170